# Simply pearls

Modern cooks often emphasize simplicity, and many wonderful recipes allow the featured ingredient to stand out without much tinkering. Take the same approach in making jewelry – sometimes the best designs require the least amount of effort. When you start with a featured ingredient as lovely as freshwater pearls, you don't need to add much to get beautiful results.

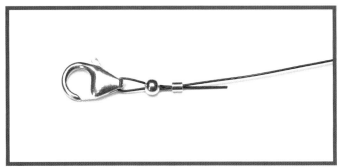

1. Measure your wrist, add 5 in. (13cm), and cut a piece of beading wire to that length. String a crimp bead, a round spacer, and the clasp. Go back through the round spacer and the crimp bead. Tighten the wire and crimp the crimp bead (see Basics, p. 19).

2. Slide a flat spacer onto the wire and over the tail. Trim the excess wire. String the pearls interspersed with flat spacers until the strand fits comfortably around your wrist. End the strand with a flat spacer.

## SupplyList

- **18–25** 8–10mm freshwater pearls, assorted shapes and colors
- **6–10** 3–4mm flat spacers
- **2** 3mm round spacers
- flexible beading wire, .014 or .015
- lobster claw clasp and 5mm split ring or soldered jump ring
- **2** crimp beads
- chainnose or crimping pliers
- diagonal wire cutters

3. To finish the bracelet, string a crimp bead, a round spacer, and the split ring or soldered jump ring. Go back through the round spacer, crimp bead, and flat spacer. Tighten the wire and crimp the crimp bead. Trim the excess wire.

*by Anne Nikolai Kloss*
*Contact Anne at annekloss@mac.com.*

# Summer simplicity

Rounds, rondelles, and bugles make this necklace a great accessory that's easy to make. All the elements are available in a multitude of colors; classic silver and apple green are but two of your options. So make a variety and have fun.

**1.** Determine the finished length of your necklace. (These necklaces are 16 in. and 18 in./41cm and 46cm, respectively.) Add 6 in. (15cm) and cut a piece of beading wire to that length. Alternate six rhinestone rondelles with five round beads on the wire. Center the beads on the wire.

## SupplyList

- **5** 8–10mm round beads
- **6** 6–7mm rhinestone rondelles
- 3g size 3 (6mm) twisted bugle beads
- **4** 2–3mm round spacers
- flexible beading wire, .014 or .015
- **2** crimp beads
- lobster claw clasp and soldered jump ring
- chainnose or crimping pliers
- diagonal wire cutters

**2.** String an equal number of bugle beads on each end until the necklace is within 1 in. (2.5cm) of the desired length.

*by Yvette Jones*
*Contact Yvette at Chic Designs by Yvette, (914) 450-3046 or yvettejonesdesigns@hotmail.com, or visit yvette-jones.com.*

**3.** On one end, string a round spacer, a crimp bead, a spacer, and the clasp. Go back through the beads just strung and tighten the wire. Repeat on the other end, substituting a jump ring for the clasp. Check the fit, and add or remove beads from each end if necessary. Crimp the crimp beads (see Basics, p. 19) and trim the excess wire.

# Drops of light

Drops of light, like tears of joy, are an unexpected pleasure. These lovely earrings use minimal time and materials to maximum effect.

**1.** Cut two 1-in. (2.5cm) pieces of wire. On one wire, make a plain loop (see Basics, p. 19) at one end. String a button crystal and make a plain loop above the crystal. On the other wire, make a plain loop at one end. String a bicone crystal and make a plain loop above the crystal.

**2.** Open a jump ring (Basics). String a crystal briolette.

## SupplyList

- **2** 13mm crystal briolettes, top drilled
- **2** 6mm button crystals
- **2** 4mm bicone crystals
- 4 in. (10cm) 24-gauge half-hard wire
- 2½ in. (6.4cm) chain, 2–3mm links
- **2** 4mm jump rings
- pair of earring wires
- chainnose pliers
- roundnose pliers
- diagonal wire cutters

**3.** Cut two ½-in. (1.3cm) pieces of chain. Attach one piece to the briolette unit. Close the jump ring. Open a plain loop on the button unit and attach the other end of the chain. Close the loop. Open the other loop on the button unit and attach the second piece of chain. Close the loop. Attach the bicone unit to the chain. Open the loop on an earring wire. Attach the dangle and close the loop. Make a second earring to match the first.

by Lea Rose Nowicki
*Contact Lea in care of Kalmbach Books.*

# Well rounded

Round out your wardrobe with a perennial favorite. Hoop earrings with dainty crystal briolettes and seed beads add a finishing touch. Universally flattering, they're a top pick for no-fuss accessorizing.

**1.** Cut a 4½-in. (11.4cm) piece of wire. Wrap it around a film canister or other round object.

**2.** Alternate seven briolettes with six 8º seed beads on the wire. Center the beads on the wire.

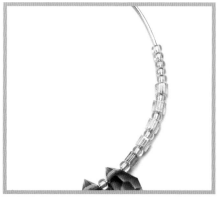

**3.** On each end, string an alternating pattern of five 11ºs and five 8ºs. String five 11ºs.

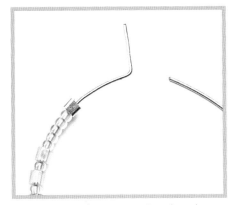

**4.** On one end, string a crimp bead and crimp it (see Basics, p. 19). Approximately ½ in. (1.3cm) from the end, bend the wire up. File the end.

**5.** On the other end, trim the excess wire to ¼ in. (6mm) and make a plain loop (Basics).

## SupplyList

- **14** briolettes, approximately 6 x 10mm
- 1g 8º hex-cut seed beads
- 1g 11º seed beads
- 9 in. (23cm) 22-gauge half-hard wire
- **2** crimp beads
- chainnose pliers
- roundnose pliers
- diagonal wire cutters
- metal file or emery board
- 35mm-film canister or other round object
- crimping pliers (optional)

*by Maria Camera*
*Contact Maria in care of Kalmbach Books.*

# Cube-a-licious

These cube-shaped beads are available in a smorgasbord of colors and are sure to become one of your favorites. By blending a four-color palette of cubes and a handful of accent beads, an easygoing necklace can be yours in no time.

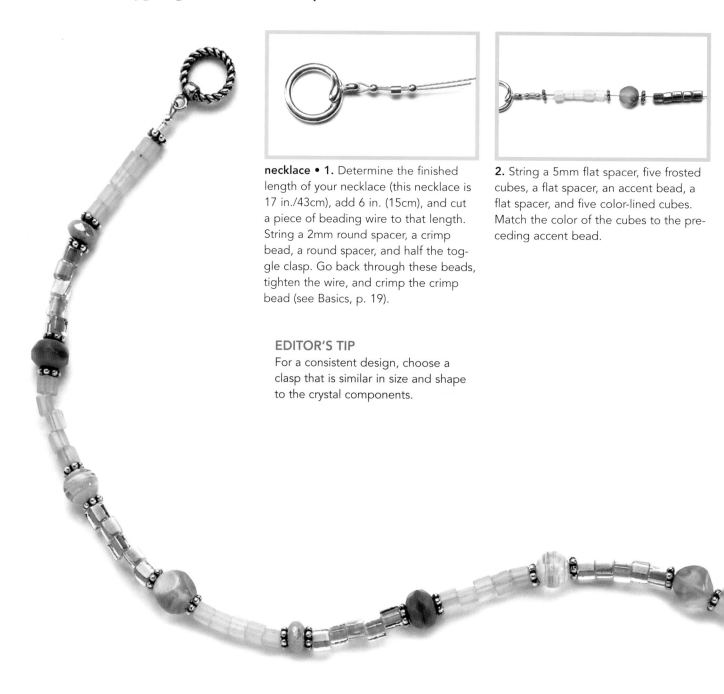

**necklace • 1.** Determine the finished length of your necklace (this necklace is 17 in./43cm), add 6 in. (15cm), and cut a piece of beading wire to that length. String a 2mm round spacer, a crimp bead, a round spacer, and half the toggle clasp. Go back through these beads, tighten the wire, and crimp the crimp bead (see Basics, p. 19).

**2.** String a 5mm flat spacer, five frosted cubes, a flat spacer, an accent bead, a flat spacer, and five color-lined cubes. Match the color of the cubes to the preceding accent bead.

### EDITOR'S TIP
For a consistent design, choose a clasp that is similar in size and shape to the crystal components.

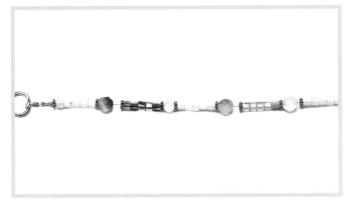

**3.** Repeat the pattern shown until you are within ½ in. (1.3cm) of your desired length. End with a flat spacer. Check the fit and add or remove beads as necessary. Finish the necklace as in step 1 with the other half of the toggle clasp.

**bracelet** • Determine the finished length of your bracelet, add 5 in. (13cm), and cut a piece of beading wire to that length. Follow steps 1 through 3 of the necklace. You may want to use fewer cubes in your bracelet pattern so you can incorporate all the colors used in the necklace.

# Supply List

**both projects**
- flexible beading wire, .014 or .015
- chainnose or crimping pliers
- diagonal wire cutters

**necklace**
- 4mm frosted cube-shaped beads, 5g each of 2 colors
- 4mm color-lined cube-shaped beads, 5g each of 2 colors
- **12** 4–8mm accent beads, **3** each of 4 colors to match cubes
- **26** or more 5mm flat spacers

- **4** 2mm round spacers
- **2** crimp beads
- toggle clasp

**bracelet**
- leftover 4mm frosted cube-shaped beads
- leftover 4mm color-lined cube-shaped beads
- **12** 4–8mm accent beads **3** each of 4 colors to match cubes
- **14** or more 5mm flat spacers
- **4** 2mm round spacers
- **2** crimp beads
- toggle clasp

*by Anne Nikolai Kloss*

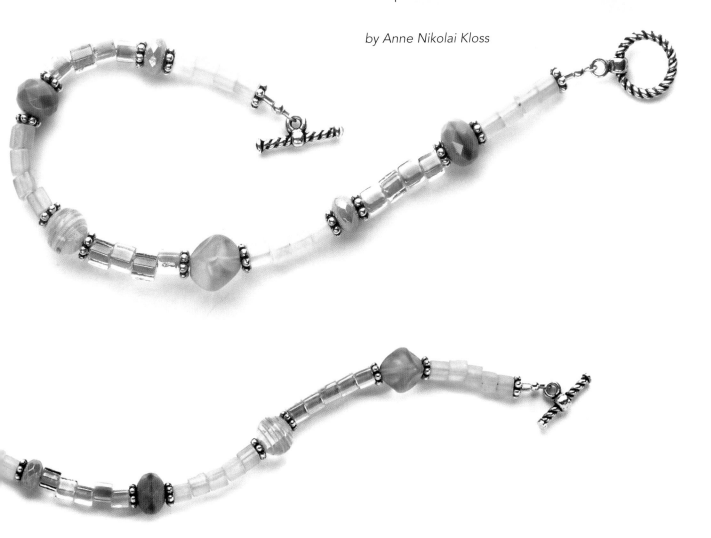

# Easy briolette
## bracelet

A strand of briolettes can often be costly; this quick bracelet showcases their beauty without too much expense or effort. Alternating the position of the briolettes creates a scalloped silhouette, while teardrop pearls complement the curves. Add a pair of pearl earrings for classic, unencumbered style.

**bracelet • 1.** Determine the finished length of your bracelet, add 5 in. (13cm), and cut a piece of beading wire to that length. String briolettes until the bracelet is half the desired length. Center the briolettes on the wire and position them in opposite directions, as shown.

**2.** String pearls on each end until the bracelet is within 1 in. (2.5cm) of the desired length.

**EDITOR'S TIP**
To add less length to the bracelet, string 4mm crystals, rather than pearls, on each end.

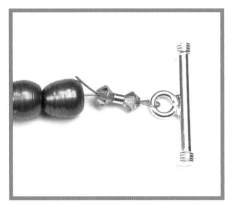

**3.** On each end, string a crystal, a crimp bead, a crystal, and half of the clasp. Go back through the beads just strung and tighten the wires. Check the fit, and add or remove an equal number of beads from each end if necessary. Crimp the crimp beads (see Basics, p. 19) and trim the excess wire.

**4.** String a pearl, a flat spacer, and a crystal on a head pin. Using the largest part of your roundnose pliers, make the first half of a wrapped loop (Basics).

**5.** Attach the dangle's loop to the loop half of the clasp. Complete the wraps.

**earrings • 1.** String a pearl, a flat spacer, a crystal, and a round spacer on a head pin. Make a wrapped loop above the spacer.

**2.** Open an earring wire loop and string the dangle. Close the loop. Make a second earring to match the first.

*by Judy Pifko*
*Contact Judy at pifko@shaw.ca.*

# Supply List

**bracelet**
- **9–13** 13mm briolettes
- **7–11** 8mm pearls
- **5** or more 4mm bicone crystals
- 4–5mm flat spacer
- flexible beading wire, .014 or .015
- 1½-in. (3.8cm) 24-gauge head pin
- **2** crimp beads
- toggle clasp
- chainnose pliers
- roundnose pliers
- diagonal wire cutters
- crimping pliers (optional)

**earrings**
- **2** 8mm pearls
- **2** 4mm bicone crystals
- **2** 4–5mm flat spacers
- **2** 2mm round spacers
- **2** 1½-in. (3.8cm) 24-gauge head pins
- pair of earring wires
- chainnose pliers
- roundnose pliers
- diagonal wire cutters

# Long&short
## of it

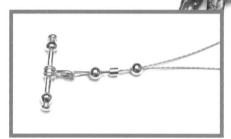

Freshwater stick pearls come in a variety of colors, and no two are exactly alike. Their long, narrow, irregular form is called *baroque*, and like music of the same name, stick pearls are elegant and classy. Mix stick pearls and round pearls in this refined cuff.

**1.** Determine the finished length of your bracelet, add 5 in. (13cm), and cut a piece of beading wire to that length. String a round spacer, crimp bead, round spacer, and one clasp section. Go back through the beads and tighten the wire, but do not crimp the crimp bead yet.

**2.** String three flat spacers, three stick pearls, a flat spacer, a round pearl, and a flat spacer. Then string two stick pearls, a flat spacer, a round pearl, and a flat spacer. Repeat, starting with the three stick pearls, until the bracelet is the desired length.

## SupplyList

- **15** or more freshwater stick pearls
- **16** or more 6mm flat spacers
- **5** or more 6mm round pearls
- **4** 3mm round spacers
- **2** crimp beads
- flexible beading wire, .014 or .015
- toggle clasp
- chainnose or crimping pliers
- diagonal wire cutters

**3.** String three flat spacers, a round spacer, a crimp bead, a round spacer, and the remaining clasp section. Go back through the beads and tighten the wire. Check the fit. Add or remove an equal number of beads from each end, if necessary. Tighten the wires, and crimp the crimp beads (see Basics, p. 19). Trim the excess wire.

*by Beth Stone*
*Contact Beth at bnshdl@msn.com or (248) 855-9358, or visit bethstone.com.*

# Win a silver metal

String a contemporary bracelet and earrings that pair puffy disks with tiny, pale crystals. Alternate printed and matte beads; you'll love the juxtaposition of graphic patterns and smooth silver.

*by Nina Cooper*
*Visit ninadesigns.com for materials and more great projects.*

**bracelet • 1.** Determine the finished length of your bracelet, add 5 in. (13cm), and cut a piece of beading wire to that length. String a printed bead, a crystal, a matte bead, and a crystal. Repeat until the bracelet is within 1 in. (2.5cm) of the desired length. End with a printed or matte bead.

**2.** On each end, string a spacer, a crimp bead, a spacer, and half of the clasp. Go back through the beads just strung and tighten the wire. Check the fit, and add or remove beads if necessary. Crimp the crimp beads (see Basics, p. 19) and trim the excess wire.

**earrings • 1.** On a decorative head pin, string a crystal and a printed bead. Make the first half of a wrapped loop (Basics) above the top bead.

**2.** Attach the dangle to the loop of an earring wire. Complete the wraps. Make a second earring to match the first.

# Just in time

You can never have too many watches. This two-strand, silver-accented band has the look of a bracelet instead of a conventional watchband. This project works up so quickly, you'll be able to make one in less than 30 minutes.

**1.** Cut 18 in. (46cm) of beading wire. String a 3mm flat spacer, a crimp bead, a 3mm round spacer, and the watch face.

**2.** Go back through the beads, tighten the wire, and crimp the crimp bead (see Basics, p. 19). Trim the excess wire.

**3.** String a pattern of beads as shown, or design one of your own. Continue stringing beads until the beaded section wraps comfortably around your wrist twice. Allow at least 2½ in. (6.4cm) of wire for finishing.

**4.** String a 3mm round spacer, a crimp bead, a 3mm round spacer, and the clasp. Go back through the beads, tighten the wire and crimp the crimp bead. Trim the excess wire.

To fasten the watch, attach the lobster claw clasp to the available watch face loop.

*by Gloria Farver*
*Contact Gloria at rfarver@wi.rr.com.*

## SupplyList

- **9** beads, 8–10mm, assorted shapes and colors
- **9–10** 8–10mm silver beads
- **18–20** 4mm crystals
- **20** 3mm round silver spacers
- **34–38** 3mm flat spacers
- watch face with one loop on each side
- **2** crimp beads
- lobster claw clasp
- flexible beading wire, .014 or .015
- chainnose or crimping pliers
- diagonal wire cutters

# Fashion
## statement

A black-and-white necklace is the perfect accessory to bridge your wardrobe from winter to spring. Dalmatian jasper offers a subtle combination of creamy white and muted black, and the rainbow obsidian pendant lends an air of elegance to this classic design.

**1.** Determine the finished length of the inner strand of your necklace (this necklace is 18½ in./47cm), add 6 in. (15cm), and cut a piece of wire to that length. Cut a second wire 2½ in. (6.4cm) longer.

Center the focal bead on the longer wire. On each side, string an alternating pattern of one crystal and one 8mm bead, until your necklace is within 1 in. of your desired length.

**3.** String a 6mm bead, a 3mm spacer, a crimp bead, a spacer, and half the clasp on each strand on both ends. Go back through the last beads strung.

**4.** Check the fit and add or remove beads as necessary. Tighten all four wires and crimp the crimp beads (see Basics, p. 19). Trim the excess wire.

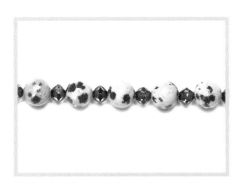

**2.** On the shorter wire, string an alternating pattern of 6mm beads and crystals, stopping when you are about 1 in. short of your desired length.

## Supply List

- 10 x 30mm (approx.) focal bead
- 16-in. (41cm) strand 8mm round gemstones
- 16-in. strand 6mm round gemstones
- **96** 4mm crystals
- **8** 3mm round spacers
- **4** crimp beads
- flexible beading wire, .014 or .015
- clasp
- chainnose or crimping pliers
- diagonal wire cutters

*by Karin Buckingham*
*Karin is an associate editor at Kalmbach Books. Contact her at kbuckingham@ kalmbach.com.*

# Facets of distinction

Faceted nuggets polished to a glossy sheen are bold and enticing. But for some, the cumbersome nature of a chunky necklace outweighs its beauty. No need to resist these tempting morsels any longer. Use the nuggets front and center to keep them as the focus, but alleviate the bulk. Finish your necklace with smaller beads accompanied by deeply hued crystals to preserve the necklace's heavyweight impact.

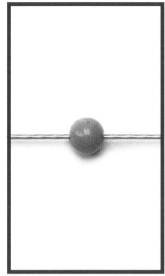

**1.** Determine the finished length of your necklace including the dangle. (This necklace is 19 in./48cm plus a 3-in./7.6cm dangle.) Add 10 in. (25cm) and cut a piece of beading wire to that length.

Center a 3mm round bead on the wire.

**2.** Fold the wire in half around the 3mm bead. On both strands, string an 8mm spacer, a nugget, a 3 x 2mm spacer, an 8mm round, a 3 x 2mm spacer, a nugget, and a crystal.

**3.** Separate the wires. On each end, string a crystal, a nugget, a crystal, an 8mm spacer, a crystal, and a nugget.

**4.** On each end, string a crystal, an 8mm spacer, and a crystal.

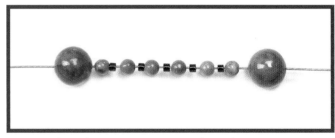

**5.** On each end, string an 8mm round, an alternating pattern of six 3mm rounds and five cylinder beads, and an 8mm round.

**6.** Repeat steps 4 and 5 until the necklace is within 1 in. (2.5cm) of the desired length.

**7.** On each end, string a 2mm round spacer, a crimp bead, a 2mm round spacer, and half the clasp. Go back through the beads just strung and tighten the wire. Check the fit, and add or remove an equal number of beads from each end if necessary. Crimp the crimp beads (see Basics, p. 19) and trim the excess wire.

*by Paulette Biedenbender*

*Paulette is the owner of Bead Needs in Hales Corners, Wisc. Contact her at (414) 529-5211, or visit beadneedsllc.com.*

## Supply List

- 16-in. (41cm) strand faceted agate nuggets (eBeadShop, 770-696-5321, ebeadshop.com)
- 16-in. strand 3mm round beads, rhodochrosite
- **15** 8mm round beads, rhodochrosite
- **23** 4mm bicone crystals
- 1g size 11º Japanese cylinder beads
- **11** 8mm spacers with a 4mm hole
- **2** 3 x 2mm spacers
- **4** 2mm round spacers
- flexible beading wire, .014 or .015
- **2** crimp beads
- hook-and-eye clasp
- chainnose or crimping pliers
- diagonal wire cutters

# Chic nuggets

What do you do when you have style to spare but no time to waste? Put together a couple of leftover nuggets and simple spacers for a smart, classic necklace.

**1.** String a spacer and a nugget on a head pin. Make the first half of a wrapped loop (see Basics, p. 19) above the nugget.

**2.** Cut a 3-in. (7.6cm) piece of wire. Make the first half of a wrapped loop at one end. String a nugget and a spacer. Make a wrapped loop above the spacer.

**3.** Attach both nugget units to a 4mm soldered jump ring. Complete the wraps.

## SupplyList

- **2** nuggets in different shapes, approximately 15 x 20mm
- **2** 5mm round spacers
- **3** in. (7.6cm) 22-gauge half-hard wire
- **18–22** in. (46–56cm) cable chain, 5–6mm links
- **2-in.** (5cm) head pin
- **8mm** jump ring
- **2** 5mm jump rings
- **4mm** soldered jump ring
- lobster claw clasp and 8mm soldered jump ring
- chainnose pliers
- roundnose pliers
- diagonal wire cutters

**4.** Determine the finished length of your necklace. (This necklace is 18 in./46cm.) Cut a piece of chain to that length. Open an 8mm jump ring (Basics). Attach the dangle to the center link of the chain and close the jump ring.

**5.** Check the fit, and trim chain from each end if necessary. Use a 5mm jump ring to attach the lobster claw clasp and one end of the chain. Repeat on the other end, substituting an 8mm soldered jump ring for the clasp.

*by Denae Oglesby*
*Contact Denae at oglesbyd@comcast.net.*

# Basics

## Plain loop

**1** Trim the wire or head pin ⅜ in. (1cm) above the top bead. Make a right-angle bend close to the bead.

**2** Grab the wire's tip with roundnose pliers. The tip of the wire should be flush with the pliers. Roll the wire to form a half circle. Release the wire.

**3** Reposition the pliers in the loop and continue rolling.

**4** The finished loop should form a centered circle above the bead.

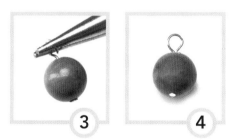

## Wrapped loop

**1** Make sure you have at least 1¼ in. (3.2cm) of wire above the bead. With the tip of your chainnose pliers, grasp the wire directly above the bead. Bend the wire (above the pliers) into a right angle.

**2** Using roundnose pliers, position the jaws in the bend.

**3** Bring the wire over the top jaw of the roundnose pliers.

**4** Reposition the pliers' lower jaw snugly into the loop. Curve the wire downward around the bottom of the roundnose pliers. This is the first half of a wrapped loop.

**5** Position the chainnose pliers' jaws across the loop.

**6** Wrap the wire around the wire stem, covering the stem between the loop and the top bead. Trim the excess wire and press the cut end close to the wraps with chainnose pliers.

## Opening and closing loops or jump rings

**1** Hold the loop or jump ring with two pairs of chainnose pliers or chainnose and roundnose pliers, as shown.

**2** To open the loop or jump ring, bring one pair of pliers toward you and push the other pair away. String materials on the open loop or jump ring. Reverse the steps to close the open loop or jump ring.

## Flattened crimp

**1** Hold the crimp using the tip of your chainnose pliers. Squeeze the pliers firmly to flatten the crimp.

**2** Tug the wire to make sure the crimp has a solid grip. If the wire slides, repeat the steps with a new crimp.

## Folded crimp

**1** Position the crimp bead in the notch closest to the crimping pliers' handle.

**2** Separate the wires and firmly squeeze the crimp.

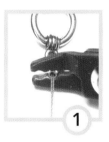

**3** Move the crimp into the notch at the pliers' tip and hold the crimp as shown. Squeeze the crimp bead, folding it in half at the indentation.

**4** Test that the folded crimp is secure.

# Get Great Jewelry Projects All Through the Year

## Your Complete Beading Resource!

### Bead&Button magazine

- New and traditional stitching techniques
- Fully-tested projects
- Step-by-step instructions and photos

### BeadStyle magazine

- Beautiful pieces in today's hottest styles
- Make jewelry in an evening or less
- Great photos and easy-to-follow instructions

## If you enjoyed *One-Hour Beading*, make sure you order these titles from the Easy-Does-It Series.

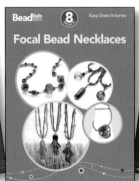

ONE HOUR BEADING

ISBN 978-0-89024-

£8.99

9 780890 246849

BKS-BDB-12344R1RH